THE
SECOND
HIGHWAY
COMPANION

Also by Harry Secombe and published by Robson Books

Harry Secombe's Highway
The Harry Secombe Diet Book
Goon Abroad: a humorous collection of travel writings
Welsh Fargo: a novel
Twice Brightly: a novel
Katy and the Nurgla: a children's story
Arias and Raspberries: the first volume of autobiography
The Nurgla's Magic Tear: a children's story

THE SECOND HIGHWAY COMPANION

presented by

Harry Secombe

in collaboration with

Ronnie Cass

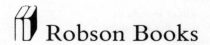 Robson Books

Designed by Harold King
Researched by Angela Pollard

First published in Great Britain in 1990 by Robson Books Ltd,
Bolsover House, 5–6 Clipstone Street, London W1P 7EB
This Robson paperback edition first published 1991

Reprinted 1991

The publisher acknowledges the help and cooperation of Tyne
Tees Television Limited and those ITV companies producing
the television series 'Highway' in publishing this book.

British Library Cataloguing in Publication Data

Secombe, Harry
  The second Highway companion.
  1. Christian life – Devotional works
  I. Title II. Cass, Ronnie
  242

  ISBN 0 86051 696 2 (cased)
  ISBN 0 86051 777 2 (pbk)

Printed and bound in Great Britain by
W.B.C. Print and W.B.C. Bookbinders,
Bridgend, Mid Glamorgan

CONTENTS

Hope

Charity

Love

Farewell (or Au revoir)

Preface

by Sir Harry Secombe

Since the first 'Highway' programme, in September 1983, I have sung hymns in fields, on a windswept jetty, in the Falklands, in stately homes, on the foredeck of the QE2, at Ben Gurion's tomb in Israel, standing on the walls of Jerusalem, with the Basilica choir in St Peter's in Rome, and in the garden of my own house. One man was always by my side, my boon travelling companion Bill Ward, the executive producer of 'Highway', and the man who did most to create it.

The Pope, the Archbishop of Canterbury, and the Archbishop of York have all given 'Highway' some of their valuable time; so have HRH Prince Philip, the Mayor of Jerusalem, the Mufti of Jerusalem, the Moderator of the General Assembly of the Church of Scotland and the lady who inspired 'the Fair Lady of Barra'.

Yet some of the finest moments on 'Highway' come from ordinary people who have done extraordinary things: Laura Morris of South Wales who fought a battle with lymphatic cancer and won, and who now helps the hospital which treated her. Jenny Rees Larcombe, the lady in a wheelchair on our programme from Burrswood, the Christian Healing centre, who spoke most movingly of how she had come to the centre

expecting a miracle and when none came, had been given the strength to bear her illness with fortitude. The list of people you have taken to your hearts is nigh on endless. People like Evelyn Glennie, the profoundly deaf Scottish lass who has gone on to become one of the finest young percussionists in the world, or Cantor Ernest Levy of Glasgow who was in eleven concentration camps during the War, and who emerged not only without bitterness but full of forgiveness. But new names have come along, not one whit less wonderful: Hilary McDowell of Donagadhee, whose parents were told at her birth that she would never walk and has since gone on not only to walk, but to become Deaconess of her local Presbyterian Church, where far from looking for help for herself, she extends help to others. Or Hilary Wilmer, one of the landladies of Nightstop in Leeds (you'll read more about Nightstop later). Or Doreen Trust, who runs the Disfigurement Centre in Cupar, of whom I remember saying at the end of the programme which came from there: 'Not one week goes by without 'Highway' amazing me; this week's amazement is the fact that a small town like Cupar is leading the country when it comes to helping people with disfigurement.'

These, and people like them, are the ones who make 'Highway' what it is, a programme about caring and inspiration. Nowhere is the caring and inspiration reflected more than in the readings which are an important part of every programme.

Ronnie Cass, Angela Pollard and myself have spend many pleasurable and nostalgic hours looking again through literally hundreds of 'Highway' programmes to select those readings which we hope will bring the most comfort and inspiration to you.

Certainly, if you receive them as you received the readings contained in the first 'Highway' Companion,

we'll be more than satisfied.

I must add a 'P.S.' to this preface. It's a sincere thank you to Kate Neely in the 'Highway' office who not only typed the whole manuscript, but also corrected the sometimes adventurous spelling and eccentric grammar she encountered.

Creation

I think I'm the lucky one, and the reason is obvious: I can spend a great part of the year travelling all over this wonderful land of ours, as well as my holiday time abroad. I am definitely getting the best of both worlds. After comparing the two, I have a question for all you people who rush unhesitatingly overseas every chance you get. Do you realize what you're missing at home?

This thought comes to mind when I think of 'Highway's' visit to Exmoor. (For the statisticians among you the date was the 11 February 1990.) And that's another interesting point: although it was wintertime, the beauty of Exmoor was unimpaired, though clearly different from the way it looks in springtime or summer. It's truly an all-the-year-round holiday area to be explored and relished. I remember starting the programme by singing Vivian Ellis' unforgettable song 'This Is My Lovely Day', and I venture to suggest it's never been sung against a more spectacular background.

A local poet – John Crisford – went to live there well over ten years ago, and he read for us his poem, 'Were

I a Giant', which summarizes his love of Exmoor.
  I can't resist quoting these four lines which, to me,
sum up Exmoor:

> Were I a giant, I'd bestride
> the Exmoor hills from side to side,
> and with my great all-seeing eyes
> look down upon this paradise.

WERE I A GIANT

Were I a giant, I'd bestride
the Exmoor hills from side to side,
and with my great all-seeing eyes
look down upon this paradise

and trace the Exe, the tumbling Lyn,
the silver chain of Winsford's Winn,
the gentle Barle, and nameless streams
that light dark combes with sudden gleams.

I'd watch the great black cattle stand
as if fast-rooted to the land
and smile at fields uncommon steep
bespattered white with countless sheep,

and see men work with plough and spade,
or sit with cider in the shade,
or walk enmeshed in sorrow's moods,
or lie in love in secret woods.

Were I a giant, I'd bestride
the Exmoor hills from side to side,
and with my great all-seeing eyes
look down upon this paradise
and stoop, and fondly touch the sea,
and kiss the cairn on Dunkery.

John Crisford

*I*n May 1989, I visited Washington. No, not that one, a much older one: Washington in the north of England. But there is a connection between the two, because Washington Old Hall was the ancestral home of the first president of America, George Washington himself, over two hundred years ago. At the same time, I was also able to meet again, after a long gap in time, an old friend from 'Oliver!' – Shani Wallis, who played the part of Nancy in the film.

But enough of this preamble, he said.

I'm here to tell you about the reading, which very appropriately was delivered by TV's vet, Christopher Timothy. Appropriate, because the subject was to do with animals. A reading which proves conclusively the old saying, there's nothing new under the sun. It's an excerpt from the novel *The Brothers Karamazov* and was written by Dostoevsky in the years 1879–80, well over a hundred years ago. But to be honest, if I hadn't told you that, couldn't you easily have imagined it was written by any of today's conservationists?

LOVE OF LIFE

Lord, may we love all your creation, all the earth and
every grain of sand in it. May we love every leaf,
every ray of your light.

May we love the animals: you have given them the
rudiments of thought and joy untroubled. Let us
not trouble it; let us not harass them, let us not
deprive them of their happiness, let us not work
against your intent. For we acknowledge unto you
that all is like an ocean, all is flowing and blending,
and that to withhold any measure of love from
anything in your universe is to withhold that same
measure from you.

Adapted from Fyodor Dostoevsky's
The Brothers Karamazov

*B*eamish Open Air Museum in Tyne Tees territory is a museum with a difference. It portrays, in detail, life in the early 1900s in that part of England.

In our 'Highway' from there in November 1988 I met up with an old friend (well, I am the godfather of her eldest son), Wendy Craig. Wendy has been on 'Highway' more than once, but particularly she was on a 'Highway' programme where I was more than a little nervous. I had good reason to be, the date of the programme was November 1983, and it was the very first 'Highway' filmed. At Beamish, Wendy read for us this lovely poem written by Armorel Kay Walling—'Go tell all creatures in the world'.

I also remember my visit to Beamish for another very good reason. I sang a new song there; a song I predict is destined to become a standard; a song with excellent words and memorable music. You thought so too, that's why I've included it in this book, in the chapter on 'Faith.' Oh . . . I nearly forgot to tell you the name of the writer of the song . . . Wendy Craig.

GO TELL ALL CREATURES IN THE WORLD

Go tell all creatures in the world
The Good News that I bring;
That was the message Jesus gave,
And He is Lord and King.

Let's tell it by the deeds we do;
In ways they understand:
Deal gently with the beasts and birds
Who share our Saviour's land.

Protect His forests, heal the air,
Care for His shining sea,
Arrest our cruelty and greed
And set its victims free.

So shall our lives proclaim the One
Who sent a little child
To lead all things safe home, in Him
Redeemed and reconciled,

To where – upon His holy hill –
None hurt and none destroy
And all Creation's present groans
Are turned to songs of joy.

Armorel Kay Walling

There's a lyric writer I particularly admire—his name is David Climie. He wrote what I consider to be the definitive song about Scotland. It's called 'A Land For All Seasons', and I've sung it many times on 'Highway'. There's one line in it I think is poetic magic:

'The silent explosion of green that is spring'.

Nothing evokes Scotland to me as much as this song. He has now written a new one for me about Wales that I know I'm going to enjoy just as much.

This long preamble is merely to say that I do enjoy poetry that is evocative; poetry that stirs the memory buds.

Here's a poem that does exactly that. It concerns the period of our lives we never forget no matter how old we become—our childhood.

It was written and read for us by James Ellis in our programme from Bangor.

I defy you to read 'Supper at Seven' without memories of your own childhood flooding through you.

SUPPER AT SEVEN

As scenes from my childhood unfold in my mind –
Long hours by the seaside, whole days on the sands –
There's grey rocks, and white horses, a wild sky
    behind,
A stretch of dark shore where a tall pine tree stands;
Across the broad ocean, the dim Scottish hills,
Above me loud seabirds with bright orange bills;
And there's twelve hours of freedom till supper at
    seven –
Sure there's fish in the water, and God's in his heav'n!

Beyond in the glen a great cataract roars,
Over rocks and round pebbles the stream struggles
    free;
As high overhead the gaunt cormorant soars,
It will carve out a course to the beckoning sea.
But the sun's barely risen, the day's just begun,
The dog's at your feet and right ready to run,
And the world is your oyster, and God's in his
    heav'n –
And the time is your own until supper at seven.

Now evening draws in, though you don't feel the cold,
But the dog is dog-tired, and you're nigh on your
   knees;
And it's time to return like the sheep to the fold,
By the scent of the sea-wrack that's borne on the
   breeze.
As you round the last bend you're in sight of Aunt
   Jean's,
And you catch that aroma of bacon and beans –
Yes, you're right on the nail for your supper at seven,
All's well with the world – and God's in his heav'n!

James Ellis

Who will forget the forbidden reading of our youth. The tuppenny boys' comics like the *Hotspur*, the *Wizard*, *Magnet* and the *Rover*. Well, in addition to these I was totally fascinated by the adventure novels of H. Rider Haggard. (Even the name sounded extraordinary and filled with promise of great tales to be told.) He was always known as H. Rider Haggard, and it was many years before I found out that the H stood for Henry.

He was most famous for his books on Africa, books like the often-filmed *King Solomon's Mines*, and the thrilling *She*.

Rider Haggard was born in Norfolk, the sixth son of a Norfolk Squire, and 'Highway' was in Norfolk when our reading was provided by John Timpson.

What has all this to do with Rider Haggard, you are probably asking? Well the reading came from 'A Norfolk Notebook', and was written by one Lilias Rider Haggard, who turned out to be the daughter of my childhood author hero.

The description of the Norfolk marsh is as vivid and colourful as you could wish, and I'm sure that it would have earned a nod of approval and a pat on the back from her father.

'GREY AND SUNLESS IT MAY HAVE BEEN'

Grey and sunless it may have been, but the marsh was full of colour. The pale masses of sedge, thick and soft as cream-coloured fur. The brilliant emerald patches of young grass round the pools of flood water. The browns and umbers and golds of the reeds, standing with the dark-plumed heads all leaning one way, like the sheaves which bowed down to Joseph, the light shining silver along the spear point of their leaves. Grey November and the thraldom of winter's hand upon the land. The cry of the redshank and the distant snarl of the tide on the shingle. The long line of woods and rounded hills behind, the pewter-grey sea ahead – this corner of England which, once it holds your heart, is more lovely than any place on earth.

Lilias Rider Haggard, from 'A Norfolk Notebook'

*L*et me tell you about a memorable interview I had on the 'Highway' visit to Jersey. Then I'll introduce a reading from somewhere else – from Sunderland in fact. The reason is because I think the two interconnect beautifully.

The interview was with Gerald Durrell at his zoo in Jersey. A zoo dedicated to the conservation of endangered animals throughout the world. Immediately the interview started a limia – an animal only to be found in the wild on the island of Madagascar – leapt onto my shoulder. I started off by asking Gerald what animals he had there at his zoo, and he replied happily, 'Oh we've got everything. What would you like to be bitten by?'

In a more serious vein, he said that as far as mankind is concerned, all things are possible. Paraphrasing the great American naturalist William Reed, he said that as far as mankind is concerned, while it is possible another Mozart or Rembrandt might be born, any species of animal once lost is lost forever. Right on cue at these words the limia leapt from my shoulder.

I was reminded of this conversation when I again came across the poem selected by Maxwell Deas at Sunderland for his reading. (It was lovely to welcome Max back on 'Highway' in this new capacity. He was Head of Religious Programming at Tyne Tees when 'Highway' was launched and now, after in excess of thirty years in television, he is enjoying a well-earned retirement. Knowing Max, that will mean he is working harder than before his retirement.)

The poem 'The Sandpiper' was written by Celia Thaxter, and it contains these memorable lines concerning the sandpiper:

> I do not fear for thee, though wroth
> The tempest rushes through the sky;
> For are we not God's children both
> Thou, little sandpiper and I?

I know that Gerald Durrell would approve of those lines.
So for that matter would the leaping limia.

THE SANDPIPER

Across the narrow beach we flit,
One little sandpiper and I,
And fast I gather, bit by bit,
The scattered driftwood bleached and dry.
The wild waves reach their hands for it,
The wild wind raves, the tide runs high,
As up and down the beach we flit –
One little sandpiper and I.

Above our heads the sullen clouds
Scud black and swift across the sky.
Like silent ghosts in misty shrouds
Stand out the white lighthouses high.
Almost as far as eye can reach
I see the close-reefed vessels fly,
As fast we flit along the beach –
One little sandpiper and I.

I watch him as he skims along,
Uttering his sweet and mournful cry.
He starts not at my fitful song,
Or flash of fluttering drapery.
He has no thought of any wrong;
He scans me with a fearless eye:
Staunch friends are we, well tried and strong,
The little sandpiper and I.

Comrade, where wilt thou be tonight
When the loosed storm breaks furiously:
My driftwood fire will burn so bright!
To what warm shelter canst thou fly?
I do not fear for thee, though wroth,
The tempest rushes through the sky;
For are we not God's children both,
Thou, little sandpiper and I?

Celia Thaxter

he 8 October 1989 was a very special Sunday for me. 'Highway' visited Hereford, and the reason it was so special was because it was the 250th 'Highway'. It was hard to believe it. Reaching programme 250 after being originally signed to do twelve.

It was a time for celebration and I was delighted to share that time with two of my oldest friends in the business: Beryl Reid and Roy Castle.

Beryl provided the reading, a poem by a former Poet Laureate, John Masefield. It's a poem which I think has a very important message. As we look around the world and witness the conflicts and starvation, it is easy to become gloomy and forget that God's purpose in creating life was to make us appreciate his wonders.

Masefield's poem, 'Laugh and Be Merry' enjoins us that enjoyment is not only necessary, but is also, in its own way, a virtue to be practised.

LAUGH AND BE MERRY

Laugh and be merry, remember, better the world with
a song,
Better the world with a blow in the teeth of a wrong.
Laugh, for the time is brief, a thread the length of a
span,
Laugh and be proud to belong to the old proud
pageant of man.

Laugh and be merry: remember, in olden time,
God made Heaven and Earth for joy He took in a
rhyme,
Made them, and filled them full with the strong red
wine of mirth,
His
The splendid joy of the stars: the joy of the earth.

So we must laugh and drink from the deep blue cup
of the sky
Join the jubilant song of the great stars sweeping by,
Laugh, and battle, and work, and drink of the wine
outpoured
In the dear green earth, the sign of the joy of the Lord.

Laugh and be merry together, like brothers akin,
Guesting awhile in the rooms of a beautiful inn,
Glad till the dancing stops, and the lilt of the music
ends.
Laugh till the game is played; and be you merry my
friends.

John Masefield

Faith

In January 1989, 'Highway' went to Weardale. Historically, the area has always been involved with shipbuilding. So much so it was considered to be the home of shipbuilding, but, due to 'progress' if progress it be, it ended there in 1989 with the closure of the North East Shipbuilders Ltd.

The unexpected view of the Wear is the beautiful countryside away from the mouth of the river and industrial Sunderland.

The reading for the programme was an ancient Gaelic prayer. When I consider any prayer I always ask one question: is there anything in the actual words or the sentiment of that prayer which confines it to a specific religion?

Read this particular prayer and I think you will agree that if you apply my test you could imagine such a prayer being delivered by Christian, Moslem, Hindu, Jew or Buddhist, or any other religion, and it would not conflict with the precepts of any of them. Not a bad few lines to keep handy I would say.

'AS THE RAIN HIDES THE STARS'

As the rain hides the stars
As the autumn mist hides the hills
As the clouds veil the blue of the sky
So the dark happenings of my lot
Hide the shining of thy face from me.
Yet, if I might hold thy hand in the darkness
   it is enough.
Since I know that though I may stumble in my going
   thou dost not fall.

Gaelic prayer

*A*nd to prove I wasn't bluffing about Wendy Craig's song, here it is. You can take my word about the music, or if you're still doubtful, why not go out and buy a copy.

SHOW ME THE WAY

When I'm confused Lord,
Show me the way
Show me, show me the way.
Baffled and bruised Lord,
Show me the way,
Show me, show me the way.
Still my heart and clear my mind,
Prepare my soul to hear
Your still small voice, your word of truth:
'Peace, be still, your Lord is near.
Always so close to show you the way,
Show you, show you the way.'

When I'm afraid Lord,
Show me the way,
Show me, show me the way.
Weak and dismayed Lord,
Show me the way,
Show me, show me the way.
Lift my spirit with your love,
Bring courage, calm and peace.
You who bore all for my sake
So I could walk, from fear released;
With you beside me showing the way,
Showing, showing the way.
Showing, showing the way.

Wendy Craig

The resilience, the strength, the unconquerability of the human spirit is a continual source of wonder. No matter what 'the inhumanity of man to man', the faith and belief of those wronged remains immutable. What is even more remarkable is that such men can emerge from all their suffering entirely lacking in bitterness, and can still devote their lives to the service of others. I've already mentioned Cantor Ernest Levy in my preface, but to him you can add the Reverend Hugo Gryn of the Berkeley Street Synagogue in London. Both spent long periods in concentration camps but their belief and faith remained unimpaired. These words – read in our programme from the Channel Islands – in a programme whose theme was faith, were written on the wall of a cellar hideout in Germany during the Holocaust. The author remains unknown. Just three lines, but they say it all.

'I BELIEVE IN THE SUN'

I believe in the sun when it is not shining
I believe in love when feeling is not
I believe in God even when he is silent.

Author Unknown

To say one has faith is comparatively easy. In most cases there is no sure way that faith can be put to the test. After all it is ultimately just a statement. St Paul in his Epistle to the Hebrews describes people who *have* been put to the test, people forced to turn their backs on home and go into the unknown, with only their faith to sustain them.

This passage from the Epistle to the Hebrews was read for us by Edith MacArthur in our programme from the Isle of Arran.

'AND WHAT IS FAITH?'

And what is faith? Faith gives substance to our hopes, and makes us certain of realities we do not see. It is for their faith that the men of old stand on record.

By faith Abraham obeyed the call to go out to a land destined for himself and his heirs, and left home without knowing where he was to go. By faith he settled as an alien in the land promised him, living in tents, as did Isaac and Jacob, who were heirs to the same promise. For he was looking forward to the city with firm foundations, whose architect and builder is God.

All these persons died in faith. They were not yet in possession of the things promised, but had seen them far ahead and hailed them, and confessed themselves no more than strangers or passing travellers on earth. Those who use such language show plainly that they are looking for a country of their own. If their hearts had been in the country they had left, they could have found opportunity to return. Instead, we find them longing for a better country – I mean, the heavenly one. That is why God is not ashamed to be called their God; for he has a city ready for them.

And what of ourselves? With all these witnesses to faith around us like a cloud, we must throw off every encumbrance, every sin to which we cling, and run with resolution the race for which we entered, our eyes fixed on Jesus, on whom faith depends from start to finish.

St Paul's Epistle to the Hebrews
Chapters 11 and 12

There was a very brilliant President of the United States named Benjamin Franklin. He had the wonderful knack of expressing great wisdom in homely aphorisms. Aphorisms that have long outlived him. For instance, who has not heard this at some time in their lives: 'A little neglect may breed mischief . . . For want of a nail the shoe was lost; for want of a shoe the horse was lost; for want of a horse the rider was lost; for want of a rider the battle was lost.' And all for the want of a nail.

You mightn't think so, but those words have a great affinity with the underlying theme of a truly religious poem written by Rudyard Kipling called 'Eddi's Service'.

In it Kipling beautifully brings forth the very comforting fact that we all of us, from the very humblest upward, have a part to play in the great overall plan of the Almighty.

EDDI'S SERVICE

Eddi, priest of St Wilfrid
In his chapel at Manhood End,
Ordered a midnight service
For such as cared to attend.

But the Saxons were keeping Christmas,
And the night was stormy as well
Nobody came to the service,
Though Eddi rang the bell.

'Wicked weather for walking'
Said Eddi of Manhood End.
'But I must go on with the service
For such as care to attend.'

The altar-lamps were lighted,
An old marsh donkey came,
Bold as a guest invited,
And stared at the guttering flame.

The storm beat on at the windows,
The water splashed on the floor,
And a wet, yoke-weary bullock
Pushed in through the open door.

'How do I know what is greatest,
How do I know what is least?
That is my Father's business,'
Said Eddi, Wilfrid's priest.

'But three are gathered together –
Listen to me and attend.
I bring good news, my brethren!'
Said Eddi of Manhood End.

And he told the ox of a manger
And a stall in Bethlehem,
And he spoke to the ass of a rider,
That rode to Jerusalem.

They steamed and dripped in the chancel,
They listened and never stirred,
While, just as though they were Bishops
Eddi preached them the Word.

Till the gale blew off on the marshes
And the windows showed the day,
And the ox and the ass together
Wheeled and clattered away.

And when the Saxons mocked him,
Said Eddi of Manhood End,
'I dare not shut His chapel
On such as care to attend.'

Rudyard Kipling

Woe and alack! The truth must be faced. Welsh Rugby is in decline, certainly at the time I write this. (The end of the 1989–90 season.) We don't seem to have the knack of producing outside halves off the assembly line as we did in the glorious days of Barry John, Cliff Morgan, and Phil Bennett. They were – in the vernacular – something else.

But one who would have qualified as a Welsh outside half was the magical Irish footballer Tony Ward, which is why I was so happy to meet him when 'Highway' went to Carlingford. Tony read for us from St John, chapter 14, verses 1–7. These are words that surely were designed to bring comfort. As you may know, actors have the habit of trying to grab off the best lines for themselves, so forgive me if I quote:

In my Father's house are many mansions.
If it were not so, I would have told you
I go to prepare a place for you.

'LET NOT YOUR HEART BE TROUBLED'

'Let not your heart be troubled. Ye believe in God, believe also in me. In my Father's house are many mansions: if it were not so, I would have told you. I go to prepare a place for you. And if I go and prepare a place for you, I will come again, and receive you unto myself; that where I am, there ye may be also. And whither I go you know, and the way ye know.' Thomas saith unto him, 'Lord, we know not whither thou goest; and how can we know the way?'

Jesus saith unto him, 'I am the way, the truth, and the life; no man cometh unto the Father, but by me. If ye had known me, ye should have also known my Father also: and from henceforth ye know him and have seen him.'

St John, chapter 14: verses 1–7

In a quiet Buckinghamshire market town called Olney, I learned a great deal about the life of the poet William Cowper. It was in many ways a sad life. His mother died when he was only six, and Cowper never really got over that.

Cowper sufferd severe depressions but found solace in his love of animals. Spiritually, he was helped by John Newton, a quite amazing man: born in 1725, he had finally become a devoted Christian after at one time being involved in the Slave Trade. A man who will never be forgotten if just for the fact that he wrote that sublime hymn, 'Amazing Grace'.

Cowper suffered a severe breakdown, and came to the conclusion that there was no salvation for him. But he also decided that this was the way his faith was to be tested.

His philosophy in the face of his trials and tribulations is to be found in one of the most famous hymns ever written. 'God Moves in A Mysterious Way'. What an expressive and meaningful title, with a faith that could be summed up in these four lines:

> Judge not the Lord by feeble sense,
> But trust him for his grace;
> Behind a frowning providence
> He hides a smiling face.

'GOD MOVES IN A MYSTERIOUS WAY'

God moves in a mysterious way
His wonders to perform;
He plants his footsteps in the sea,
And rides upon the storm.

Deep in unfathomable mines
Of never-failing skill
He treasures up his bright designs,
And works his sovrain will.

Ye fearful saints, fresh courage take,
The clouds ye so much dread
Are big with mercy, and shall break
In blessings on your head.

Judge not the Lord by feeble sense,
But trust him for his grace;
Behind a frowning providence
He hides a smiling face.

William Cowper

The essence of faith is ultimately simple. It is acceptance without proof. To say one will believe if a sign is given is to negate the whole essence of true belief. Yet so many of us are constantly looking for that sign. The sign that will strengthen and fortify.

Possibly where we lack courage is to admit we think that way. Here is a poem that deals with that anguish. A thinking poem, a poem painfully honest. In it you can feel the innate desire to believe, but also not to be afraid to speak of the difficulties encountered along the way. The reading comes from a most unusual setting, Armley prison in Leeds. It was written by a prisoner there, and read by Jenny Barnes who is training to be an assistant Chaplain in the prison.

The prisoner finds the peace he prays for in these lines:

I ask for forgiveness please let me come home,
This soul in life's wilderness a sheep far from home.

PRAYER OF
A CONFUSED
CHRISTIAN

Oh, to sleep your eternal sleep,
Called to my Maker's bosom,
Lay to rest my earthly chains,
Which bind me so tight,
And dim my sight, such pleasures to forgo,
Are nothing compared with eternal grace,
These temptations of the human race,
I long to be at one with my creator God
I have walked so long this lonely dark.

In youth and childhood belief comes easily
In middle age confusion leaps from me
Each path seems wrong, the clock ticks on,
Tick Tock, Tick Tock, life's passing by.
Must it be Church Lord, steeped in tradition,
Its meaning lost to me like a relic,
Must we meet in your house Lord,
The thought which I abhor
House of the righteous, pious and sane,
Not of the curious, confused, insecure.
I know in my heart there's more to me,
A right side, a good side, you seldom see . . .
I speak to you often, half-heartedly.
Please give me an answer, a sign to read,
I know deep inside me I carry your seed.

I ask for forgiveness please let me come home,
This soul in life's wilderness a sheep far from home.
Please hear me and give me a sign
I wish to share Lord the love that is Thine.

God is good,
God is merciful,
God is forgiveness,
God is pity,
God is everything in me that is good.
God is love, but I don't understand Him!

A 'Lifer', HM Prison Leeds, Christmas 1989

A friendly rivalry exists between 'Highway' and 'Songs of Praise'. Not too unexpectedly, after all we transmit at the same time – Sunday at 6.40 – we are both religious programmes, and so we are competing for the same audience.

But I do emphasize that the rivalry is friendly, although some good-natured joshing does go on. For instance, whenever we are out shooting a 'Highway' programme and are held up by the noise of passing aircraft, this is always referred to as Thora Hird piloting the 'Songs of Praise' plane. But the ultimately good relations existing between us and the BBC could not have been more clearly illustrated than in our programme on the 22 October 1989.

The programme came from Morecambe Bay, and we were quite delighted to have as our guest a lady who had been born there, none other than the star of 'Praise Be' herself, Thora Hird.

After talking together, Thora read a very famous piece, 'Footsteps in the Sand'. I think it's known to many, but it took a 'Highway' viewer, Iris Element of Bucknall in Berkshire, to draw it to our attention.

A salutary reminder for those who might on occasions doubt the love of God.

P.S. Of course. The answer is simple. Why didn't I think of it before? I'm going to fly the 'Highway' aeroplane and disturb the 'Songs of Praise' recordings.

FOOTSTEPS IN
THE SAND

One night a man had a dream. He dreamed he was walking along the beach with the Lord. Across the sky flashed scenes from his life. For each scene, he noticed two sets of footprints in the sand: one belonging to him, and the other to the Lord. When the last scene of his life flashed before him, he looked back at the footprints in the sand. He noticed that many times along the path of his life there was only one set of footprints. He also noticed that this happened at the very lowest and saddest times of his life.

This really bothered him and he questioned the Lord about it: 'Lord, you said that once I decided to follow you, you would walk with me all the way. But I have noticed that during the most troublesome times of my life, there is only one set of footprints. I don't understand why when I needed you most you would leave me.'

The Lord replied: 'My precious, precious child, I love you and I would never leave you. During your times of trial and suffering, when you see only one set of footprints, it was then that I carried you.'

Anon

Hope

There is an author I much admire, who, sadly I think, is not nearly as well known as he should be. That even though he has been described as the greatest Scottish writer of the century, and even though his books have been dramatized on TV in such series as 'Sunset Song'.

His name is Lewis Crassic Gibbon, and he was a mere thirty at the time of his death. In our programme from Stonehaven in Grampian territory, the actress Vivien Heilbron, who was famous for her interpretation of Gibbon's words, read for us an excerpt from 'Sunset Song'.

It is in the form of an epitaph for four men from that part of the world, Kinraddie to be exact, who died in the Great War. Beautifully as Vivien read it, the quality of the writing and the ideas flowing through it can only be fully assimilated after numerous readings, as you are bound to find.

It produces mixed emotions; there is a pervading sadness expressed in such lines as:

They died for a world that is past, these men,
but they did not die for this that we seem to inherit.

But overall there is an exhortation that bids us to struggle that they did not die in vain.

This reading sent me scurrying for more Lewis Crassic Gibbon. Perhaps it will do the same for you.

EXCERPT FROM 'SUNSET SONG'

For I will give you the morning star. In the sunset of an age and an epoch we may write that for epitaph of the men who were of it. They went quiet and brave from the lands they loved, though seldom of that love might they speak, it was not in them to tell in words of the earth that moved and lived and abided, their life and enduring love. And who knows at the last what memories of it were with them. The springs and the winters of this land and all the sound and scents of it that had once been theirs, deep, and a passion of their blood and spirit, those four who died in France?

Nothing, it has been said, is true but change, nothing abides, and here in Kinraddie where we watch the building of those little prides and those little fortunes on the ruins of the little farms we must give heed that these also do not abide, that a new spirit shall come to the land with the greater herd and the great machines. For greed of place and possession and great estate those four had little heed, the kindness of friends and the warmth of toil and the peace of rest – they asked no more from God or man, and no less would they endure.

They died for a world that is past, these men, but they did not die for this that we seem to inherit. Beyond it and us there shines a greater hope and a newer world, undreamt when these four died. But need we doubt which side the battle they would range themselves did they live today, need we doubt the answer they cry to us even now, the four of them, from the place of the sunset?

Lewis Crassic Gibbon

arly in 1989, 'Highway' went to Yeovil, and it was there that the actress Sheila Allen read for us some words of T.S. Eliot. When you consider what has happened to Eliot since his death, the words are uncannily prophetic.

He surely could never have dreamt that he would supply the libretto for a 'smash-hit' musical; and yet with the musical *Cats*, that is exactly what he has done. A musical not merely successful in this country but the world over. In the light of that just consider these words of Eliot:

> And to make an end is to make a beginning.
> The end is where we start from.

Words that must strengthen our faith in the eternity of things, our belief in the reality of a life hereafter. As a modest writer myself I cannot help but adore Eliot's own attempts to achieve a perfectionism in his own writing:

> . . . And every phrase
> And sentence that is right (where every word
>   is at home
> Taking its place to support the others.
> The word neither diffident nor ostentatious,
> An easy commerce of the old and the new. . .

> And so on.
>   It reminds me of that lovely line by Alexander Pope:
> 'What oft was thought, but ne'er so well expressed.'

EXCERPT FROM 'LITTLE GIDDING'

What we call the beginning is often the end
And to make an end is to make a beginning
The end is where we start from. And every phrase
And sentence that is right (where every word is at
    home
Taking its place to support the others.
The word neither diffident nor ostentatious,
An easy commerce of the old and the new,
The common word without vulgarity,
The formal word precise but not pedantic,
The complete consort dancing together).
Every phrase and every sentence is an end and a
    beginning
Every poem an epitaph. And any action
Is a step to the block, to the fire, down the sea's throat
Or to an illegible stone: and that is where we star.
We die with the dying:
See, they depart, and we go with them.
We are born with the dead:
See, they return, and bring us with them.
The moment of the rose and the moment of the
    yew-tree
Are of equal duration. A people without history
Is not redeemed from time, for history is a pattern
Of timeless moments. So while the light fails
On a winter's afternoon, in a secluded chapel
History is now and England.

T.S. Eliot

*N*ear New Year in 1984, 'Highway' visited Edinburgh, and there I met one of the most remarkable characters ever to come on the programme. Her name is Carolyn James, and she seemed to be a contradiction in terms. Let me explain: in her late thirties, Carolyn went blind, the inevitable consequence of Retinitus pigmentosa. Yet it was only after the onset of her blindness that Carolyn developed her creative ability. This was the main topic of the conversation I had with her, because amazingly Carolyn had chosen to express her creativity by becoming a watercolour artist. (The fact that she is now a formidable watercolour artist is not the most important point, the fact that she had the courage and determination to paint at all is. Not only remarkable, you must think, but well- nigh impossible.)

If you want to learn more about how it's done then read Carolyn's recently published book *Images In The Dark*. But Carolyn's painting is not the main part of this story. Because soon after meeting her, I learned that our talk had caused her great frustration. The reason was that in her handbag she had been carrying a further example of her creative ability (again one developed since the advent of her blindness), some song lyrics she thought might suit me, but she lacked the courage to show. Finally, egged on by a friend, she sent them to my office. They impressed me tremendously, so much so I passed them on to my music man of 'Highway', and my co-author – Ronnie Cass. The net result was that very shortly afterwards, in a 'Highway' from Dunfermline,

I sang the first of many Carolyn James songs I was to sing; it was called 'A Little Understanding'.

Soon afterwards, from Stamford, Lorna Dallas sang another Carolyn James song, 'Paint My Life'.

Knowing now what you do of Carolyn, read the lyric. It is not only beautiful in its own right, but also expresses the courage that can be brought to bear to overcome the handicap of blindness, and yet still show appreciation for the beauty of the world around us.

PAINT MY LIFE

Now take the sunshine from the sky
And the breezes passing by
And don't ask for reasons why
Just paint my life.

Now take the autumn's misty chill
And a lonely windy hill
Take a river running still
And paint my life.

Take the sound of horses' hooves
Take the snow from cottage roofs
Try really try –
Let your mind touch clouds on high
Just so long as you paint my life.

Now take the words that make you wise
Take the tears and take the sighs,
Take the love that never dies,
And paint your life.

Now take the beauty of a kiss
Take the moments that you miss
Take the magic of all this,
And paint your life.

Carolyn James

*T*he theme of our programme from Stamford was beauty. If I may be allowed to quote myself, I remember saying in that 'Highway', 'Beauty is not just the preserve of fine places and sophisticated people. It's for you and me.' If you ever think of anything to do with beauty, then John Keats' famous poem *Endymion* must spring to mind, although most people know it by its first line: 'A thing of beauty is a joy for ever.' What is not so well known – and I am indebted to our indefatigable researcher, Angela Pollard, for this little gem – is that Keats was a Cockney, a thoroughgoing Cockney at that. So, if he were reciting his own poem it might well start: 'A fing of beauty is a joy for ever'.

If you'd like to make a note, Mr Lionel Bart, you'll learn that, 'Fings *were* what they used to be'.

But frivolity on one side, enjoy and enjoy again this superb poem which was read for us in Stamford by James Faulkner.

EXCERPT FROM 'ENDYMION'

A thing of beauty is a joy for ever:
Its loveliness increases; it will never
Pass into nothingness, but still will keep
A bower quiet for us, and a sleep
Full of sweet dreams, and health,
And quiet breathing.
Therefore, on every morrow,
   are we wreathing
A flowery band to bind us to the earth,
Spite of despondence,
of the inhuman dearth
Of noble natures, of the gloomy days,
Of all the unhealthy and o'er-darkened ways
Made for our searching: yes,
In spite of all.
Some shape of beauty moves away the pall
From our dark spirits.

John Keats

*J*oy and sorrow have often been considered two sides of a coin, and if they are it follows that you can't have the one without the other.

Here are two readings that warn us that we must be prepared to accept the ups and down of life. The first one is from the book *The Prophet* by Kahlil Gibran. It came from our programme from Harlow New Town and acted as a palliative to a particularly harrowing interview I had just completed. It was read for us by Caroline John.

The second reading is in the form of a prayer, read for us by Penelope Lee, and came from our programme from the Britannia Royal Naval Training College in Dartmouth.

I particularly like the lines:

> The winds that blow over us
> are the breathing of thy Spirit
> the sun that lights and warms us
> is Thy Truth.

EXCERPT FROM 'THE PROPHET'

Then a woman said, 'Speak to us of Joy and Sorrow'.
And he answered:
'Your Joy is your Sorrow unmasked. And the selfsame well from which your laughter rises was oftentimes filled with your tears.
And how else can it be?
The deeper that sorrow carves into your being, the more joy you can contain.
Is not the cup that holds your wine the very cup that was burned in the potter's oven?
And is not the lute that soothes your spirit the very wood that was hollowed with knives?
When you are joyous, look deep into your heart and you shall find it is only that which has given you sorrow that is giving you joy.
There are those who give with joy, and that joy is their reward.
And there are those who give and know not pain in giving, nor do they seek joy, nor give with mindfulness of virtue; through the hands of such as these God speaks, and from behind their eyes He smiles upon the earth.'

Kahlil Gibran

'ALMIGHTY FATHER, THY LOVE IS LIKE A GREAT SEA'

Almighty Father, Thy love is like a great sea that girdles the earth.
Out of the deep we come to float awhile upon its surface.
We cannot sound its depth, nor tell its greatness,
only we know it never faileth.
The winds that blow over us are the breathing of Thy Spirit;
the sun that lights and warms us is Thy Truth.
Now Thou dost suffer us to sail calm seas –
now thou dost buffet us with storms of trouble –
on the crest of waves of sorrow Thou dost raise us,
but it is thy love that bears us up –
in the trough of desolation thou dost sink us, that we may see naught but Thy love on every side.
And when we pass into the deep again the waters of Thy love encompass and enfold us.
The foolish call them the waters of misery and death;
those who have heard the whisper of Thy Spirit know them for the the boundless ocean of eternal life and love.

Anon

*I*t is well over three years since 'Highway' visited the Scilly Islands, the chosen retirement haven of ex-Prime Minister Lord Wilson. But the person who provided our reading – in all senses – was his wife, Mary Wilson.

Her subject matter was the lifeboat, and even more so the crew of the lifeboat.

Quietly courageous people who assemble, with no thought of reward, to help their fellows in trouble; because, by definition, they are not called upon unless the raging elements have proved too much for ordinary sailors, and ordinary ships, to cope with.

I said Lady Wilson provided our reading in all senses, by which I mean she not only read it, she also wrote the words. Her poem is simply entitled: 'The Lifeboat'.

THE LIFEBOAT

We hear the rocket from the slip
Fast, fast we run to watch them go
Here in the dark we only know
That Scilly Rock has claimed a ship.

We see them as we cross the strand –
The smiling boatmen from the quay
Stern oil-skinned strangers seem to be
Passing the ropes from hand to hand.

Old Matt looks on with wistful face
He's had his share of risks and fears –
Coxswain or crew for sixty years –
And now young Matt stands in his place.

Now Doctor Bell climbs in the boat
The pulleys turn, the cables lift
Into the water, smooth and swift
One rush of spray, and she's afloat.

Thank God there is no fog tonight
But tearing gale and streaming rain
No stars to guide her home again
Only the steady harbour light.

The evil rock waits in the gloom
Crouched like a beast beneath the waves
Careless of all the lives she saves
Eager to trick her to her doom.

A bobbing cork beside the wreck
They cast a line to pull her in
Half-deafened by the tempest's din
Which roars above the slippery deck.

And we can only stand and pray
And as the chilly hours creep by
Watch for the paling of the sky
How long it seems to wait for day!

Is that her engine? Yes, at last
'All's well, all safe!' we hear them shout
She edges in, and comes about
Her journey done, her danger past.

Mary Wilson

When 'Highway' made an Easter special from Westminster Abbey, one of the areas we couldn't miss looking at was Poets' Corner. An area that all visitors to the Abbey make sure of seeing. Among the most famous of Britain's writers and poets buried there is Charles Dickens – possibly the most popular of all.

Dickens wrote a book especially for his own children on the life of Jesus called *The Life Of Our Lord*, and we were lucky to have that noted actor John Woodvine to read an excerpt from it dealing with the events of Easter Sunday.

It got me to thinking.

How wonderful to have a father who was a consummate story-teller. Certainly so in the case of Dickens, an author who travelled the world giving readings from his own works. So his children not only received private readings, but were also guaranteed star performances to go with them. I can just picture the scene with Dickens reading his latest story with his children gathered round.

Almost as good as having a toymaker for a father, and an endless supply of new toys coming off the assembly line. I'm not complaining you understand, but looking back, I can't remember an occasion when my own children requested a lullaby to put them to sleep. Cowards, all of them – afraid to face the decibels. Compared to me, they used to think Tom Jones's voice was gentle and soothing.

EXCERPT FROM 'THE LIFE OF OUR LORD'

When that morning began to dawn, Mary Magdalene and the other Mary, and some other women, came to the Sepulchre with some more spices which they had prepared. As they were saying to each other, 'How shall we roll away the stone?' the earth trembled and shook, and an angel, descending from Heaven, rolled it back, and then sat resting on it. His countenance was like lightning, and his garments were white as snow; and at the sight of him, the men of the guard fainted away with fear, as if they were dead.

Mary Magdalene saw the stone rolled away, and waiting to see no more, ran to Peter and John who were coming towards the place, and said, 'They have taken away the Lord and we know not where they have laid him!' They immediately ran to the Tomb, but John, being the faster of the two, outran the other, and got there first. He stooped down, and looked in, and saw the linen clothes in which the body had been wrapped, lying there; but he did not go in. When Peter came up, he went in, and saw the linen clothes lying in one place, and a napkin that had been bound about the head, in another. John also went in, then, and saw the same things. Then they went home, to tell the rest.

But Mary Magdalene remained outside the Sepulchre, weeping. After a little time, she stepped down, and looked in, and saw two angels, clothed in white, sitting where the body of Christ had lain. These said to her, 'Woman, why weepest Thou?' She answered, 'Because they have taken away my Lord, and I do not know where they have laid Him.' As she gave this answer, she turned round, and saw Jesus standing behind her, but did not then know Him. 'Woman,' said He, 'why weepest thou? what seekest thou?' She, supposing Him to be the gardener, replied, 'Sir! If thou hast borne my Lord hence, tell me where thou hast laid Him, and I will take Him away.' Jesus pronounced her name, 'Mary.' Then she knew him, and, starting, exclaimed 'Master!' – 'Touch me not', said Christ; 'for I am not yet ascended to my father; but go to my disciples, and say unto them, I ascend unto my Father, and your Father, and to my God, and to your God!'

Charles Dickens

Charity

We might not like to face the fact, but the overwhelming majority of us tend to think too much about ourselves. Possibly true unselfishness is what distinguishes the saintly from the rest of us. So a timely reminder to 'love thy neighbour' does not come amiss.

The message from our Ipswich programme in May 1987 provided exactly that. It was read by an actress called Georgie Glen who was working at the local Ipswich Theatre. She impressed us all greatly, and I was pleased to learn that she has since gone on to the National Theatre.

I really like the reading, and its central message can apply to all of us, 'stop worrying about your own halo and shine up your neighbour's'!

CIRCLE OF LIGHT

One Sunday morning, drowsing in the back pew of a little country church, I dimly heard the old preacher urge his flock to 'stop worrying about your own halo and shine up your neighbour's!' And it left me sitting up, wide-awake, because it struck me as just about the best eleven-word formula for getting along with people that I ever heard.

I like it for its implication that everyone, in some area of life, has a halo that's worth watching for and acknowledging. I like it for the picture it conjures up: everybody industriously polishing away at everybody else's little circle of divine light. I like it for the firm way it shifts the emphasis from self to interest in and concern for others. Finally, I like it because it reflects a deep truth: people have a tendency to become what you expect them to be.

Arthur Gordon

*T*hose of you who remember the first 'Highway' Companion will remember how, when we thought the book was ready to be 'put to bed' – as the publishing term goes – we had a late reading which produced such an outburst of letters and telephone calls we had no hesitation in including it in the book as a sort of P.S.

Well here's another piece from the same writer and book, *The Prophet* by Kahlil Gibran and I make not the slightest apology for including in *this* book a second excert from *that* book. It was read for us in St Athan, by Roy Marsden. The subject is 'giving', and the truth of Gibran's writing is such as to make us all that little bit uncomfortable.

As a totality it can teach us much, but if we can just remember one sentence, the lesson it teaches will have served its purpose.

It is well to give when asked, but it is
better to give unasked...

EXCERPT FROM 'THE PROPHET'

Then said a rich man, 'Speak to us of giving.'
And he answered:

There are those who give a little of the much which they have — and they give it for recognition and their hidden desire makes their gifts unwholesome.
And there are those who have little and give it all. These are the believers in life and the bounty of life, and their coffer is never empty.

It is well to give when asked, but it is better to give unasked, through understanding.
And to the open-handed the search for one who shall receive is joy greater than giving.

And is there aught you would withhold?
All you have shall some day be given; therefore give now, that the season of giving may be yours and not your inheritors'.

You often say, 'I would give, but only to the deserving'.
The trees in your orchard say not so, nor the flocks in your pasture. They give that they may live, for to withhold is to perish.
Surely he who is worthy to receive his days and his nights is worthy of all else from you.
And he who has deserved to drink from the ocean of life deserves to fill his cup from your little stream.

Kahlil Gibran

I'll tell you about a group of people who easily
fulfil the total definition of charity and giving
as previously defined by Kahlil Gibran.

I'm not for moment suggesting these people are
unique, but I felt proud and privileged to have met
them on our 'Highway' from Leeds.

The organization is called 'Nightstop', and the people
who run it go well beyond giving time and money. They
open their doors and provide a home and love, as well
as hot food and a warm bed to youngsters who would
otherwise be sleeping rough. If you were to tell these
people they were winning the plaudits of Kahlil Gibran
or fulfilling so fully the words of Matthew, chapter 25
verses 35–40 – they would probably give you a very
puzzled look.

The verses from Matthew were very movingly read
by Sister Mary Catherine at the Convent of the Little
Sisters of the Poor.

'I WAS HUNGRY'

I was hungry and you fed me,
thirsty and you gave me a drink;
I was a stranger and you received me in your home,
naked and you clothed me;
I was sick and you took care of me,
in prison and you visited me.

The righteous will then answer him,
'When, Lord, did we ever see you hungry and feed
   you,
or thirsty and give you a drink;
When did we ever see you a stranger
and welcome you in our homes,
or naked and clothe you?
When did we ever see you sick,
or in prison and visit you?'
The King will reply, 'I tell you,
whenever you did this for one
of the least important of these brothers of mine,
you did it for me.'

St Matthew, chapter 25: verses 35–40

We pray for so many things. Sometimes our prayers can be selfish as we plead for something only for ourselves, something purely material. More often, prayers are offered up by one on behalf of another. A prayer for continued good health, or for the successful outcome of an operation. But of all forms of prayer surely none can be more incredible than one offered on behalf of an oppressor.

The reading that follows comes from Sue Ryder's autobiography, *Child of My Love*. (I know I have no need to tell you of the wonderful work performed by Sue and her husband Group Captain Leonard Cheshire since the end of the war; particularly the 'Living Memorial', which is the Sue Ryder Foundation.)

It was a prayer that had obviously influenced her greatly, a prayer written originally by Sir Thomas More. The power of the prayer was such that a copy of it was found on the body of a young child who died in Ravensbruck concentration camp.

No more appropriate time for the reading of the words could have been found than in our 1988 Remembrance Day programme from Suffolk and the Stour Valley.

A PRAYER

O Lord, remember not only the men and women of goodwill, but also those of ill-will. But do not only remember all the suffering they have inflicted on us, remember the fruits we bought thanks to this suffering, our comradeship, our loyalty, our humility, the courage, the generosity, the greatness of heart which has grown out of all this, and when they come to judgement, let all the fruits we have borne be their forgiveness.

Sir Thomas More

*I*f you want to find out how to solve all the world's problems, big and small, from world peace to the problem of parking, there's one sure place to look – the correspondence columns of newspapers. All newspapers, from local publications through to the national dailies.

We've all read such letters, maybe some of us have even written them. I'm not pooh-poohing, because occasionally such a letter can lead to action that can be long-lasting and effective over many years.

A perfect example is a letter read on our programme from Quarrier's village.

In fact the main subject matter of the programme could be said to have originated as a direct consequence of this letter. Certainly it gave rise to the creation of Quarrier's village, and, appropriately, the village is named after the writer of the letter – William Quarrier. The letter was addressed to the Editor of the *Glasgow Herald*, and – make note of the date – it was written in 1871.

It was read for us by Bill McCue, who regards himself, along with all the inhabitants of the village, as one of Quarrier's children.

LETTER TO THE
EDITOR OF THE
GLASGOW HERALD,
AUGUST 1871

Sir,

For many years past I have been deeply impressed with the necessity that exists here for a Home for destitute boys, of whom 1,137 either roam our streets or country without a home to cheer their desolate lives, or a house to cover their defenceless heads.

Some have an easy way of getting out of their Christian responsibilities, and they say of these helpless ones, 'Send them to the Poorhouse'; others, to quiet their consciences, give a copper when they see the haggard face and tattered garments of the little street urchin, and so the stream of neglected children goes on, deepening and deepening until God only knows what length it may reach.

Fellow Christians and fellow citizens, should such things continue? I would say no, and thus I plead for a Home to which any boy may be sent, his case enquired into, and a helping hand extended to him. Shall the practical help and sympathy of my fellow-citizens be wanting? I have no faith in large institutions where hundreds are

ruled with a stringent uniformity which eats out the individuality of its members, but I have great faith in a Home where not more than one hundred would be cared for and watched over by a motherly and fatherly love. The Home might cost from £1,000 to £2,000, and if any of my fellow-citizens would feel inclined to put out this sum or any amount towards it, I feel certain that it would be laying up treasure in Heaven, where neither moth nor rust doth corrupt, and the blessing for those who are ready to perish would be sure to fall on their heads.

Yours truly

W. Quarrier

upar is a small town in Fife, Scotland. It also has an incredible tale to tell. Now I choose my word carefully. I am well aware that the word 'incredible' means 'unbelievable', and work is being done in Cupar that cannot be described with any other word than 'incredible'. Let me tell you about it.

There is an unsightly face mark which is medically known as an angioma. It strikes seemingly haphazardly, and is descriptively known as a 'port wine stain'. It can hopefully fade a little with age, but generally has been regarded as something that one must learn to live with. Something against which conventional medicine has seemed pretty unavailing. Until now, people have been prepared to accept the unhappy situation, but not Doreen Trust. A victim herself, she has devoted her life to fighting this aberration of nature. She set up the Disfigurement Guidance Centre in Cupar and by the use of lasers some significant success has been achieved. To such an extent that the little town of Cupar has become the leading centre for the fight against, and the treatment of, angioma. And not only angioma; Doreen Trust and her team are now able to offer the most advanced treatment to disfigured children, without charge, and as part of the National Health Service. Bearing all this in mind, I'm sure you'll find

the reading for this programme very apposite. It was delivered by a former pupil of Bell Baxter High School in Cupar, Professer Robert Davidson, now Moderator of the General Assembly of the Church of Scotland. It is from the Gospel of St Mark, chapter 9, verses 33–37. It contains one of the most profound of Christ's pronouncements to his disciples: 'Whoever wants to be first must place himself last of all and be the servant of all.'

'THEY CAME TO CAPERNAUM'

They came to Capernaum, and after going indoors Jesus asked his disciples 'What were you arguing about on the road?' But they would not answer him, because on the road they had been arguing among themselves about who was the greatest. Jesus sat down, called the twelve disciples to him and said to them, 'Whoever wants to be first must place himself last of all and the servant of all.'

Then he took a child, and made him stand in front of them. He put his arms around him and said to them, 'Whoever welcomes in my name one of these children, welcomes me; and whoever welcomes me, welcomes not only me but also the one who sent me.'

St Mark, chapter 9: verses 33–37

*H*istory can illuminate, but it can also horrify in its illumination. Take for instance the years 1845–9 in Ireland: those years were the years of the Irish famine, a famine caused by the potato blight. As a result of it 700,000 people died, and a million more emigrated – mainly to America.

One family who had lived through these terrible times was the Irvine family of Antrim, and it was there that a hundred years ago Alexander Irvine was born. His mother's maxim was 'love is enough', and that saying dominated his upbringing.

Her faith was exemplified by her deliberate choice of name for him, Alexander – which means 'helper of men'. Alexander certainly justified that faith by becoming, firstly a minister in New York, and later a Padre for the YMCA in the trenches during the First World War.

This famous story of Irvine, The Tinker of Tobercurry – vividly evokes the childhood conditions he endured.

It was read for us by Michael Duffy, in the little house in Antrim where Irvine was born.

THE TINKER OF
TOBERCURRY

The annual fair day in Antrim was a great occasion for the poor. The main street was lined with stalls which were crowded with gingerbread and candy. Merchants came from far and near to display their wares. 'Farmhands' changed their masters or made new contracts on that day and hiring was done in the open street.

It was a great day for beggars, wanderers, thimbleriggers, acrobats, conjurors and queer people who lived by their wits.

My greatest ambition was to be old enough for a farmer to lay his hand on my shoulder and ask me to serve him for the following year. It was exciting to see a farmer bargain with a boy, by spitting in his hand and slapping a shilling into the palm of the new 'farm-hand', for the following year. I think I was more enamoured with the prospect of three meals a day than I was with agriculture.

On the eve of every fair we had a 'stranger within our gates'. They were at home where night found them. We never asked their names. We never knew their occupations, if they had any. We were afraid to know. They were welcome to a 'bit and a sup', of whatever we had and the privilege of curling themselves up in our corner for the night, on the mud floor, or sitting in front of the peat fire. They were all good story-tellers

and we regretted we had so little to give in return.

'God save all here', said a shaggy-looking man one night as he walked in and looked us over. 'God save ye kindly,' said my mother. 'I get my bread by the grace of God an' speyin' fortunes', said the man. 'I'm here to turn an honest penny at the fair th' morrow.'

It was about nine in the evening. We had hoped for a potato supper but the hope had died and all we had was a pot of tea to go in six directions. We gathered around the fire and the stranger was given his share.

'Maybe, ye toss th' cups?' said my mother. 'As aisy as readin' th' face ov a clock,' he replied. He twirled his cup around three times then placed it mouth down on the saucer. The first picture he saw in the struggling tea leaves made our mouths water. It was a Belshazzar feast of choice viands quite foreign to our wildest imaginings. How these things were to arrive or who should provide them were details too unimportant to mention. We would have been quite satisfied with a pot of porridge, or a potato each, but our faith was equal to the picture.

Eventually, we all stole quietly away to our beds so full of the stranger's stories that we forgot that we had had no supper. My pallet was in the little half-loft stretching along the edge so that as I lay on my side I could raise my head over the edge and see the stranger sitting in front of the turf fire. I was quite sure that the man was a fairy – maybe the leprechaun himself. I intended to keep close watch during the night but soon went to sleep and did not waken until the grey dawn came in through the front window. I looked over the edge. The man was gone. I descended the little ladder.

As my feet felt the mud floor I saw spread out on the table viands fit for a king. There was a fried chicken, a

stack of buttered slices of bread, a big lump of mashed potatoes, and a gooseberry pie.

'Quick!' I yelled as I shook the household out of sleep. 'Come and see! The man was a fairy an' has left us wonderful things t'ate.' In a few seconds we were all in a huddle around the stuff, touching each item to see if it was real.

'From God or th' divil?' asked father looking at my mother. 'God,' she said, 'did ye think they had changed their jobs?' In that case . . .

'It must be God,' father said, 'the divil hasn't sense enough to know which is the hungriest family in th' town.'

'A good guess,' said mother, 'there's only wan thing of two to do – ate it or give it away!'

'We'll ate it,' said father and we did.

Alexander Irvine

Love

I have a favourite quotation. It is from Thomas Carlyle. He wrote:

Blessed is he who has found his work,
let him ask no other blessing.

Well I think I qualify under that heading. My work has been my pleasure, and my pleasure has been my work.

But I think I can go beyond that, because I have also had an idyllic family life. A marriage that has stayed young, fresh and adventurous, as well as loving (thank you, Myra), not to mention the nicest accoutrements of marriage: in my case four children and three grand-children (so far).

Bearing this in mind, I was delighted by the reading in our programme from Haddington, in East Lothian, a few miles from Edinburgh (on a mellow autumn day). The reason for my delight was because I was the reader of a love letter written by the above mentioned Thomas Carlyle to his wife Jane.

It was so nice to know that he too had not only 'found his work', but was also blessed by the gift of true love.

'O JEANNIE, HOW HAPPY WE SHALL BE'

O Jeannie, how happy we shall be in our new house! We shall sit under our bramble and our elder tree, and none to make us afraid; and my little wife will be there forever beside me, and I shall be well and blest. Surely I shall learn at length to prize the pearl of great price which God has given to me unworthy. Surely I already know to me the richest treasure has been awarded – the heart of my own noble Jane. Oh, Jeannie! Oh my wife! We will never part – never through eternity itself; but I will love thee and keep thee in my heart of hearts! God bless thee! Ever thine,

Thomas

Thomas Carlyle, from a letter to his wife Jane

One of the comforting things I have found on 'Highway' is that I have never talked to any scientist who has found a conflict between his scientific learning and his faith. No matter to which religion he belonged.

Dr Gordon McPhate in St Andrews was no exception. Dr McPhate is a lecturer in the medical sciences department of the University whose specialist research subject is diabetes. (I was particularly happy to meet him, being a diabetic myself, I'm never one to turn up my nose at a free consultation.)

Apart from his scholastic activities, Dr McPhate fulfils another role at St Andrews, he is one of the Anglican chaplains to the University.

On the programme, he read for us – quite splendidly – Corinthians 1, chapter 13: verses 1–8.

If there is a better exposition of how empty life is without love, I can only say I have yet to encounter it.

'I MAY BE ABLE TO SPEAK THE LANGUAGES OF MEN'

I may be able to speak the languages of men, and even of angels, but if I have no love, my speech is no more than a noisy gong or a clanging bell. I may have the gift of inspired preaching; I may have all knowledge and understand all secrets; I may have all the faith needed to move mountains – but if I have no love, I am nothing. I may give away everything I have, and even give up my body to be burnt, but if I have no love, this does me no good.

Love is patient and kind; it is not jealous or conceited or proud; love is not ill-mannered or selfish or irritable; love does not keep a record of wrongs; love is not happy with evil, but is happy with the truth. Love never gives up and its faith, hope and patience never fail. Love is eternal. There are inspired messages, but they are temporary; there are gifts of speaking in strange tongues, but they will cease, there is knowledge, but it will pass.

Corinthians 1, chapter 13: verses 1–8

*I*n October 1987 'Highway' went to Limavady. It was there we learned about a most exciting project. It was called Project Ulster. The aim was to find a number of young people – fifteen was considered the ideal age – people with leadership potential, and put them together in different environments but in direct contact with one another. The hope being that when they returned home they would maintain the friendships that had been established across the religious divide. The four main churches in Limavady worked together in sending 24 such children – 12 Catholic and 12 Protestant – to the United States.

We were encouraged to learn of the project, and in a talk with youth leader Louise Campbell, I was able to learn of its success. With this in mind I sang a hymn that could have been written as a mirror image of Project Ulster. I don't want to appear naïve about this, 'one swallow does not a summer make', but any good news to be garnered from Ulster – such as Project Ulster – deserves to be publicized.

'WE ARE ONE
IN THE SPIRIT'

We are one in the Spirit
We are one in the Lord
We are one in the Spirit
We are one in the Lord
And we pray that all unity may
One day be restored

And they'll know we are Christians
By our love, by our love
Yes, they'll know we are Christians
By our love.

We will walk with each other
We will walk hand in hand
We will walk with each other
We will walk hand in hand
And together we'll spread the news
That God is in our land

And they'll know we are Christians
By our love, by our love
Yes, they'll know we are Christians
By our love.

We will work with each other
We will work side by side
We will work with each other
We will work side by side
And we'll guard each man's dignity
And save each man's pride

And they'll know we are Christians
By our love, by our love,
Yes, they'll know we are Christians
By our love.

All praise to the Father
From whom all things come
And all praise to Christ Jesus
His only son
And all praise to the Spirit
Who makes us one.

And they'll know we are Christians
By our love, by our love,
Yes, they'll know we are Christians
By our love.

Peter Scholtes

*I*f you should tell me that Jim Hacker MP is probably the most bumbling and incompetent fictitious Prime Minister this country has ever had, I would naturally have to agree with you. I might equally claim that Jim Hacker's *alter ego*, Paul Eddington, is also one of the finest actors this country possesses, and I don't think I'd have many people arguing with that.

In fact, his skill as an actor couldn't have been more clearly illustrated than in his reading of one of the most famous pieces from Richard II, because the character he portrayed in his reading was light years away from the aforesaid Jim Hacker.

I'm not going to be as silly as to try and praise Mr W. Shakespeare. It really would be a case of exporting sand to the Sahara. I will say though that no words show such affection and pride in our land without the least hint of *braggadocio*.

'THIS ROYAL THRONE OF KINGS'

This royal throne of kings, this scepter'd isle
This earth of majesty, this seat of Mars
This other Eden, demi-paradise;
This fortress built by Nature for herself
Against infection and the hand of war;
This happy breed of men, this little world;
This precious stone set in the silver sea,
Which serves it in the office of a wall,
Or as a moat defensive to a house,
Against the envy of less happier lands;
This blessed plot, this earth, this realm, this England,
This nurse, this teeming womb of royal kings,
Fear'd by their breed and famous by their birth,
Renowned for their deeds as far from home,
For Christian service and true chivalry.

William Shakespeare, from Richard II – Act 2, scene 1

I wrote these words in the first 'Highway' companion:

Without doubt the most popular reading ever on 'Highway' was 'Death Is Nothing At All'. It was read most movingly by Bernard Cribbins on the Remembrance Day programme which came from the beaches of Normandy in November 1985.

It's funny how these things occur. We were putting the Remembrance Day programme together, and looking for a suitable reading, when a 'Highway' viewer solved the problem.

Mr L. A. Maxim of Sudbury in Suffolk wrote to us, saying that his wife loved these words written by a Canon Henry Scott Holland (1847–1918), and that they had been read by the rector at her funeral service three years previously. He hoped that they might bring comfort to others. We owe Mr Maxim grateful thanks for bringing them to our attention so that we could share them with our audience.

Nothing has changed in the three years that have elapsed since I first wrote those words. The reading still remains far and away the most popular we have ever used on 'Highway', and from all the hundreds of letters we have received the one that still brings the greatest comfort.

I make no apology for using it again and I do so for two calculated reasons: one, I know that readers of the first *Highway Companion* won't object to seeing it again, and two, I would hate to think that those of you who did not read that book may have been deprived of the comfort and solace Canon Scott Holland's words invariably bring.

'DEATH IS NOTHING AT ALL'

Death is nothing at all . . . I have only slipped away into the next room . . . I am I, and you are you . . . whatever we were to each other, that we are still. Call me by my old familiar name, speak to me in the easy way you used. Put no difference into your tone, wear no forced air of solemnity or sorrow. Laugh as we always laughed at the little jokes we enjoyed together. Play, smile, think of me, pray for me.

Let my name be ever the household word that it always was. Let it be spoken without effect, without the ghost of a shadow on it. Life means all that it ever meant. It is the same as it ever was, there is absolutely unbroken continuity. What is this death but a negligible accident? Why should I be out of mind because I am out of sight? I am just waiting for you, for an interval, somewhere very near, just around the corner . . . All is well.

Canon Henry Scott Holland (1847–1918)
Sent to us by a viewer

Our memories are not as reliable as we would like to think, and for sure, the older we become the more unreliable does our memory become. That's why I offer this advice to the younger amongst you; when something good and pleasant happens to you, make a conscious effort to deposit it in your memory bank. Remind yourself of those events often and often; in this way you'll be able to give Mister Unreliable Memory a run for his money.

I'm reminded of all this when I think back to the 'Highway' visit to Ushaw College in County Durham. The reading in the programme was delivered by John Schofield, a student of the college, now a priest. He chose to read a prayer by John Henry Newman. In this prayer, Cardinal Newman refers to something that at the time is vivid in his mind, and he prayed that he never lose the crystal clear memory of it. And how beautifully he expresses this wish:

> Oh may I never lose, as years pass away,
> and the heart shuts up,
> and all things are a burden,
> Let me never lose this youthful, eager, elastic
> love of thee.

You can apply his sentiment to love of God, or to love of man or woman in equal measure.

'I COME TO THEE, O LORD'

I come to thee, O Lord, not only because I am unhappy without thee; not only because I feel I need thee, but because thy grace draws me on to seek thee for thy own sake, because thou art so glorious and beautiful. I come in great fear, but in greater love. Oh may I never lose, as years pass away, and the heart shuts up, and all things are a burden, let me never lose this youthful, eager, elastic love of thee. Make thy grace supply the failure of nature. Do the more for me, the less I can do for myself.

John Henry Newman

The 'Highway' visit to Leeds was especially joyful for me, because it was there I met up with a great friend in the business, one I meet far too infrequently, Frankie Vaughan. He has been a star for more years than either of us cares to remember, and deservedly so.

Frank is a man of many parts and if you look behind 'The Green Door' you will find that no one devotes more of his time to good work. In Frank's case it is with the Boys' Clubs up and down the country. In fact he is a patron of the National Association of Boys' Clubs.

Very appropriately, the song that Frank sang on the programme was called 'Children'. It was poignant, moving, and redolent with truth. I well remember the bitter-sweet comfort of the lines which said:

> And it gets harder as they grow older,
> But you're growing older too,
> 'Til you're a child
> And they're looking after you.

CHILDREN

Can I talk to you about children?
We bring them into the world with love,
For you do all you can for children
But it never seems enough.
And they do things that make you wonder,
And your heart they can sometimes break,
But what a difference to your world
Those children make.

Can I talk to you about children?
For there's something I need to know,
When the time comes for them to leave you,
Is it hard to let them go?
How will they get along without you,
You ask yourself time and again,
Or is the question
How will you get along without them.

And it gets harder as they grow older
But you're growing older too,
'Til you're a child
And they're looking after you.

Can I talk to you about children –
That's all I seem to do.

Jeff Morrow

*C*ertain words tend to be overused, losing their potency in the process. 'Inspiration' is one such word. But applied to Mother Teresa no other word fits the bill. She is simply and without doubt an inspirational figure. Her work among the poor in Calcutta is well enough known without having to be detailed here. When 'Highway' visited Sunderland, Mother Teresa was the subject of a song.

It was written by Brian Hume and sung by his wife Irene, while the backing was provided by Prelude, one of the most popular groups performing around Wearside. If some of the words of the song make us feel uneasy, I've no doubt that that was what Brian Hume had in mind. For instance, can anyone give a reasoned answer to these lines?

> What kind of madness is this that I see?
> Where leaders talk always of peace;
> And millions of men making weapons of war,
> While we take our place at the feast.

MOTHER OF LOVE

She cradled the head of a young dying man
She cradled his head on her arms.
And all through the night she held on to his hand
And prayed in the sweet voice that calms.

She lives with the sick and those dying alone
She lives with the beggars and blind
And shows them that their lives mean something to
    her –
That someone to them can be kind.

Mother – mother – mother of love.

What kind of madness is this that I see?
Where leaders talk always of peace;
And millions of men making weapons of war,
While we take our place at the feast.

How many like her do the best that they can,
While so many things fall apart.
She shows us that life is the greatest of all
In silence with love in her heart.

Mother – mother – mother of love.

What does she know that I haven't yet found.
How do I know that she's right?
She may not stand with her feet on the ground,
But I know she stands in the light.

Mother – mother – mother of love.

Brian Hume and Jim Hornsby

I'm pleased to say I have lots and lots of friends, but alas, only one Nobel Prize winner among them. His name is Sir James Black, and all I will tell you is that he received his Nobel Prize for medicine.

He is a Scotsman by birth and was educated at St Andrews University. In 1989 he was chosen as Scotsman of the decade. (Scotswoman of the decade I'm delighted to say was that 'Highway' stalwart the brilliant percussionist Evelyn Glennie.) So naturally when 'Highway' visited St Andrews, we invited Evelyn and Sir James to come on the programme.

The visit brought back many memories to Sir James. Nostalgic, happy recollections of his student days there. But not merely academic memories, because it was here he met his wife Hilary.

Apart from being a formidable scientist in her own right, Hilary was also a poet of considerable talent, even though her output was not prolific.

Hilary and James shared a tremendous zest for life, treasuring each day they spent together.

Hilary was aware that her days were limited when she wrote this poem 'Autumn'. It describes so beautifully the yearning for life, and the heightened awareness of nature which comes in the face of impending death.

AUTUMN

It is Autumn now
A diffuse sun scatters the fallen leaves
I know it is my Autumn
And that winter will follow soon
I try to prolong
The golden days
By capturing a fallen leaf and enclosing it
In my album
The skeleton trees herald the winter
I envy their spare beauty
Secure in the certainty
Of another Spring

Hilary Black

Many years ago, in 1958 to be exact, there was a film that took the British public by storm. It was a World War II espionage story and was based on fact. The title of the film was 'Carve Her Name With Pride'. It tells the heroic story of Violette Szabo, a London shopgirl whose French officer husband is killed in action. She enlists as a British agent and on her second mission is captured by the Germans. She is sent to Ravensbruck concentration camp, and is finally executed, winning a posthumous George Cross for her bravery.

The star of the film was Virginia McKenna, and we were delighted to welcome her to our 'Highway' from Dundee.

There was little problem in finding the reading, because all we needed to do was use these words written by Leo Marks. The words are read as a voice-over at the very end of the film. You can consider the lyric from two standpoints and it responds to either.

You can think of it as a love poem, but equally convincingly it responds if you want to consider it as a sacred song. A measure of its greatness.

'THE LIFE THAT I HAVE'

The life that I have
Is all that I have
And the life that I have is yours.

The love that I have
Of the life that I have
Is yours and yours and yours.

A sleep I shall have
A rest I shall have
Yet death will be but a pause.

For the peace of my years
In the long green grass
Will be yours and yours and yours.

from the film
'Carve Her Name With Pride'
Leo Marks

Peace

I don't want to go on about the beauty of this land of ours, but it's hard not to when you visit places like Loch Fyne. The incredible scenery to be found there is, in a word, overwhelming.

Gil Breen read for us from Isaiah, and I can think of no more appropriate reading. Apart from paying tribute to the beauty of the earth everywhere it also gives the credit where it is due:

> He fashioned the earth and all that lives there.

But more than that, the words of Isaiah also make unsolicited promises.

> When you pass through deep waters
> I will be with you;
> your troubles will not overwhelm you.
> When you pass through fire
> you will not be burnt;
> The hard trials that come
> will not hurt you.

Promise enough to bolster any wavering faith. A comfort to all.

'GOD CREATED
THE HEAVENS'

God created the heavens and stretched them out; he fashioned the earth and all that lives there; he gave life and breath to all its people. And now the Lord God says to his servant, 'I, the Lord, have called you and given you power to see that justice is done on earth. Through you I will make a covenant with all peoples; through you I will bring light to the nations.'

Sing a new song to the Lord;
sing his praise, all the world!
Praise him, you that sail the sea;
praise him, all creatures of the sea!
Sing, distant lands and all who live there!

Do not be afraid – I will save you.
I have called you by name – you are mine.
When you pass through deep waters, I will be with
    you;
your troubles will not overwhelm you.
When you pass through fire, you will not be burnt;
The hard trials that come will not hurt you.

Isaiah, chapter 42: verses 5, 6 & 10,
and chapter 43: verses 1b & 2

I think we have a tendency to believe that it is only the older ones among us who remember the past. If proof were needed that this is not so, let me tell you of Fiona Redston. Fiona went on holiday to Normandy and saw one of the cemeteries there. Later, in a 'Highway' programme, she described the effect some eighteen months later it had on her. 'I saw rows and rows of white crosses. That sticks in a young child's mind I suppose, and stays there. Thoughts of all those young people going out there and getting killed. Really for no reason at all.'

Fiona came on our Remembrance Day programme of 1987, and I talked to her. In the course of that talk Fiona said this: 'I hope that people think more and learn more from the past, and think more of all the mistakes that other people have made, and hopefully they'll see what went wrong and why it went wrong.'

Fiona was sixteen at this time, and showed great maturity for a young person of her age.

If you agree with that, consider these words which Fiona wrote to the tune of 'Amazing Grace'. Could you credit that they were written when Fiona was only fourteen and a half?

I sang them on our Remembrance Day programme of 1987. They had a tremendous effect on our viewers, and certainly no less an effect on me.

REMEMBRANCE DAY

The young and old lie buried here
In fields where poppies grow.
Each flower that blooms
Is one life lost
In Flanders Fields of woe.

In Flanders Fields they fell and died
Each mother's son so fine.
Where poppies grow
The crosses bloom
In regimental line.

But other wars have yet been fought
Who knows the reason why
Still more the poppies
Bloom and grow
While mothers mourn and cry.

Though time and age may weary us
As we grow older yet
They'll stay for ever
Young at heart
And we shall ne'er forget.

Fiona Redston

When I was a lad there was a village with ambitions to be called a town, named Llantwit Major. This implies that there was an even smaller village called Llantwit Minor. Well, amazingly there was. I remembered all this when 'Highway' went to visit the huge air station near to the Llantwits. It was known to thousands of airmen during the war, and it's called St Athan.

On our visit there I became reacquainted with 'The Pilot's Psalm'. (I had first encountered it when we visited Gatwick Airport.) While ostensibly it is a prayer for those whose job is to do with flying (or originally sailing), it is much more than that. It is, of course, a poetic rhythmic version of the 23rd Psalm, and it possesses all of the Psalm's holiness. No plea to the Lord could ask for more than these three lines:

> Surely sunlight and starlight shall favour me
> on the voyage I take,
> And I will rest in the port of my God forever.

THE PILOT'S PSALM

The Lord is my pilot
I shall not drift.
He lighteth me across the dark waters,
He steereth me in deep channels.
He keepeth my log.
He guideth me by the star of holiness
For his name's sake.
Yea though I sail mid the thunders
And tempests of life,
I will dread no danger.
For thou art near me,
Thy love and thy care they shelter me.
Thou preparest a harbour before me
For the homeland of eternity.
Thou anointest the waves with oil,
My ship rideth calmly.
Surely sunlight and starlight shall favour me
On the voyage I take,
And I will rest in the port of my God forever.

Anon

*I*t says much for the fame of the painter John Constable that a whole chunk of land — the Stour Valley in Suffolk — is often referred to as 'Constable country'. Or to put it the other way round, if you talk about Constable country people will immediately know that you are talking about the Stour Valley.

When we visited Constable country I was lucky enough to talk to Celia Jennings, an expert on the subject of John Constable. She was able to tell me about the special — almost unique — quality of the light there. Apart from almost forcing painters to paint, it also enables photographers to produce memorable results. As photography is my hobby, I was more than happy there. But more important than telling of the light there, Celia read for us this passage from the notes of Constable. A passage which shows how Constable regarded his painting as a religious experience.

'EVERY TREE
SEEMS FULL'

Every tree seems full of blossom of some kind and the surface of the ground seems quite lovely – every step I take and on whatever object I turn my eye that sublime expression in the Scripture 'I am the resurrection and the life', etc. seems verified about me.

From the private notebook of John Constable

*I*f you ever doubt the power of religion, just read the following. It's a letter written to *The Times* in 1915, and describes the events which took place on the Western Front in France. The front where trench warfare was a way of life and death for more than four years.

This letter tells of a miracle, of how so many war weary soldiers on both sides suddenly and spontaneously laid down their arms and together celebrated, in the most primitive way, one of the holiest days in the Christian calendar. The day that celebrates the birth of Jesus.

That the war would be continued was of course inevitable, but that the one day's armistice took place at all still cannot be rationalized except in the most religious of terms.

The letter was read for us in the Chapel of Durham Cathedral by that fine actor Robert Hardy. His immediate audience was the Durham Light Infantry, and his performance totally gainsaid any extraneous histrionics. He knew in his actor's wisdom that the words said it all.

'WE HAD RATHER AN INTERESTING TIME'

We had rather an interesting time in the trenches on Christmas Eve and Christmas Day. We were in some places less than 100 yards from the Germans and held conversations with them across. It was agreed in our part of the firing line that there would be no firing and no thought of war on Christmas Eve and Christmas Day, so they sang and played to us several of their own tunes and some of ours such as 'Home Sweet Home' and 'Tipperary', etc., while we did the same for them. The regiment on our left all got out of their trenches and every time a flare went up they simply stood there, cheered, and waved their hats and not a shot was fired on them. The singing and playing continued all night, and the next day (Christmas) our fellows paid a visit to the German trenches, and they did likewise. Cigarettes, cigars, addresses, etc., were exchanged and every one, friend and foe was real good pals. One of the German officers took a photo of English and German soldiers arm-in-arm with exchanged caps and helmets. On Christmas Eve the Germans burned coloured lights and candles along the top of their trenches, and on Christmas Day a football match was played between them and us in front of the trench.

They even allowed us to bury all our dead lying in front, and some of them, with hats in their hands, brought in one of our dead officers from behind their trench so that we could bury him decently.

They were really magnificent in the whole thing and jolly good sorts. I have not a very different opinion of the Germans. Both sides have started the firing and are already enemies again. Strange it all seems, doesn't it?

From a letter to The Times – *1915*

I know it's wrong to have favourites, but even on 'Highway' we do. One of them is that impish actress Patricia Brake.

Possibly the role that endeared her most to the public was as the daughter of the incorrigible Fletcher in that masterly TV series 'Porridge'.

Patricia first appeared in an early 'Highway' from Bath, when she read for us the Ballad of the Bread Man, by Charles Causley. It was so popular with viewers that it was not only printed in the first 'Highway' book, but in the first *Highway Companion* as well.

We were delighted to welcome her back to 'Highway' for our 1989 Christmas programme from Durham Cathedral. She read for us there, Longfellow's famous poem . . . 'Christmas Bells'.

CHRISTMAS BELLS

I heard the bells on Christmas Day
Their own familiar carols play,
And wild and sweet
The words repeat,
of 'Peace on earth, good will to men!'

Till ringing, singing on its way,
The world revolved from night to day –
A voice, a chime,
A chant sublime,
of 'Peace on earth, good will to men!'

And in despair I bowed my head;
'There is no peace on earth,' I said,
'For hate is strong
and mocks the song
of peace on earth, good will to men!'

Then pealed the bells more loud and deep:
'God is not dead; nor doth he sleep!
The wrong shall fail,
The right prevail,
With peace on earth, good will to men!'

Henry Wadsworth Longfellow,
From the 'Christus' trilogy:
Christmas Bells

*T*here's a tranquillity about the Healing Centre at Burrswood that has to be experienced to be fully appreciated.

'Highway' visited there early in 1990, and while all 'Highway' visits are happy events, the special atmosphere of Burrswood made this one especially so.

What was particularly impressive for me was the way conventional medicine was able to combine with faith healing to the benefit of both.

Talk to a doctor there, and he would be voluble in praise of the therapeutic effect of faith, and the antithesis would be just as true.

John Rutter wrote a beautiful song called 'Deep Peace', it was sung for us by St Philip's Choir and lyrically reflects the tranquillity of Burrswood I referred to above.

Dylan Thomas was once asked to give a simile for the word 'soft', and he said, 'Soft as a needle slipping through water'. 'Deep Peace' I find equally expressive of the peace of Burrswood.

DEEP PEACE

Deep peace of the running wave to you
Deep peace of the flowing air to you
Deep peace of the quiet earth to you
Deep peace of the shining stars to you
Deep peace of the gentle night to you
Moon and stars pour their healing light on you
Deep peace of Christ
The light of the world to you
Deep peace of Christ to you

John Rutter

*B*ereavement touches us all at some time in our lives. That couldn't have been made clearer when the reading of 'Death is Nothing at all' was first used on a 'Highway' programme, and you wrote in your thousands to ask for copies of the words, convinced beyond doubt of the comfort they would bring you.

In 1989 our Remembrance Day programme came from Scotland, and once again we paid tribute to everyone who died in service to their country.

Rather than end the programme with just a 'Goodnight, and see you next week in. . . .', I read a poem which had been found in the pocket of Stephen Cummins, a soldier who had been killed in Northern Ireland. It was first attributed to Stephen himself, but this was found not to be the case.

It has since thought to have been written by Mary Fry, an American poet, or by Marianne Rhinehart who lives in Arizona. And in some letters sent to the 'Highway' office by Mrs Cresswell of Horley in Surrey, writing on behalf of 96-year-old Miss Reynolds, it is claimed to be the work of J.T. Wiggins, the uncle of Miss Reynolds, and an Englishman who emigrated to America.

In this instance, I can't help feeling that the question of authorship takes second place to the wonderful comforting sentiments the poem contains for all of us, but particularly to the recently bereaved.

DO NOT STAND
AT MY GRAVE

Do not stand at my grave and weep
I am not there. I do not sleep.
I am a thousand winds that blow
I am the diamond glints on snow.
I am the sunlight on ripened grain
I am the gentle autumn rain.
When you awaken in the morning's hush
I am the swift uplifting rush
of quiet birds in circled flight.
I am the soft stars that shine at night.
Do not stand at my grave and cry,
I am not there; I do not die.
So heed, hear when you awaken what I say,
I live with you and guard your way.

Author uncertain

I know every composer in the land will disagree with what I'm about to say, and as a singer I'm possibly being a traitor to the whole breed of singer, nevertheless I believe it's true. It is simply that sometimes a tune can be so beautiful, so memorable, that the lyric it has been set to can get lost in the shuffle.

Here's a case in point, a song I sang in Malta; it's called 'Prayer Perfect', and if the composer will forgive me, I'm going to give you a chance to concentrate purely on the words without the lovely music getting in the way.

PRAYER PERFECT

Dear Lord, kind Lord, gracious Lord I pray
Thou wilt look on all I love tenderly today
Rid their hearts of weariness, scatter every care
Down a wake of angel wings winnowing the air.

Dear Lord, kind Lord, gracious Lord I pray
Thou wilt look on all I love tenderly today.

Bring unto the sorrowing all release from pain
Let the lips of laughter overflow again
And with the needy, O Divine I pray
This vast treasure of content that is mine today.

Dear Lord, kind Lord, gracious Lord I pray
Thou wilt look on all I love tenderly today.

Ervine Stenson and James Riley

*T*he truly pious exude a feeling of calm and peace which is unique. Such a person is Sister Agnes. I met her on the tiny island of Fetlar in our programme from the Shetland Isles. I was so impressed by her words that I wouldn't dream of trying to remember them, when by reference to the programme I can quote them correctly:

> When I was nineteen I decided I would give up all I had, my posessions – which were not very many at that time – also my ambitions, desires and hopes in order to find, as Francis of Assisi found, the perfect joy of loving. And I found it, and I continue increasingly to find it, in the abandonment of my life to God.

And so it has been for year after year, first in a little Franciscan community in Devon, until she finally arrived in Fetlar.

One can only remain humble in the face of such humility and holiness.

Sr. Agnes chose to read for us a beautiful prayer of St Francis of Assisi, and she couldn't have chosen a more appropriate reading, because her way of life is a mirror image of the lifestyle practised by that Saint.

P.S. An ever-zealous editor has informed me that I used this reading in the first *Highway Companion*, to which my reply is, I refuse to forgo this opportunity to re-introduce Sister Agnes to all who were so impressed with her on our Scottish programme, and surely it is impossible to read the words of St Francis too often.

'LORD, MAKE ME AN INSTRUMENT'

Lord, make me an instrument of your peace;
where there is hatred, let me sow love;
where there is injury, pardon,
where there is doubt, faith,
where there is despair, hope,
where there is darkness, light,
where there is sadness, joy.

O divine master, grant that I
may not so much seek to be consoled as to console,
to be understood, as to understand,
to be loved as to love.
For it is in giving that we receive,
it is in pardoning that we are pardoned,
and it is in dying that we are born to eternal life.

Prayer of St Francis of Assisi

Farewell (or Au revoir)

Saying goodbye is never the easiest thing to do. It produces a mixture of emotions, the sadness of actual parting combined with the expectation of meeting again.

Or as the Bard put it, 'Parting is such sweet sorrow.'

I had to say goodbye to all the 'Highway' viewers at the end of the 1990 series, as I have to say goodbye to you now. But I will never be short of the words to do that nearly perfectly again. The programme came from the Isle of Barra, and it was there I was introduced to a beautiful, peaceful hymn that says it all.

So, 'til we all meet again, let the hymn say on my behalf 'God be with you'.

Goodbye.

GOD BE WITH YOU

God be with you 'til we meet again;
By his counsels guide, uphold you,
With his sheep securely fold you:
God be with you 'til we meet again.

God be with you 'til we meet again;
'Neath his wings protecting hide you,
Daily manna still provide you:
God be with you 'til we meet again.

God be with you 'til we meet again;
When life's perils thick confound you,
Put his arm unfailing around you:
God be with you 'til we meet again.

God be with you 'til we meet again;
Keep love's banner floating o'er you,
Smite death's threatening wave before you,
God be with you 'til we meet again.

J. E. Rankin

Acknowledgements

We hope the extracts in this anthology have made you want to read more; if so, the following information may prove helpful. The authors and publisher are grateful to all those who have given permission to include copyright material.

'Were I a Giant' is taken from the book of the same name by John Crisford (Nether Halse Books) with permission; 'Love of Life' is adapted from *The Brothers Karamazov* by Fyodor Dostoevsky (Penguin); 'Go Tell All Creatures in the World' by Armorel Kay Walling is published by permission of the author; 'Supper at Seven' by James Ellis is published by permission of the author; 'Grey and Sunless it May Have Been' comes from *A Norfolk Notebook* by Lilias Rider Haggard (Faber & Faber); 'Show Me the Way' is reproduced with permission of Wendy Craig and Tembo Records; 'Prayer of a Confused Christian' is reproduced with the permission of HM Prison Service; 'Little Gidding' is from *Four Quartets* by TS Eliot (Faber & Faber); 'Paint My Life' by Carolyn James is published by permission of the author and First Time Music; 'Speak to Us of Joy and Sorrow' comes from *The Prophet* by Kahlil Gibran (William Heinemann); 'Almighty Father, Thy Love is Like a Great Sea' comes from *Book of Comfort* by Elizabeth Goudge, (Fontana Books); 'The Lifeboat' is taken from *Selected Poems* by Mary Wilson by permission of the author (Hutchinson); 'Circle of Light' comes from *The Gift of Friends* by Arthur Gordon (Fleming H Revell Co, USA); 'Speak to Us of Giving' comes from *The Prophet* by Kahlil Gibran (William Heinemann); 'I Came to Thee O Lord', by John Henry Newman, comes from The *Hodder Book of Christian Prayers*, (Hodder & Stoughton); 'Children' by Jeff Morrow is published by permission

of the author; 'Mother of Love' by Brian Hume and Jim Hornsby is reproduced by kind permission of the authors; 'Autumn' belongs to the Estate of Hilary Black and is published by kind permission of Sir James Black; 'The Young and Old Lie Buried Here' by Fiona Redston (from *Remembrance Day*) is published by kind permission of the author; 'Every Tree Seems Full' is taken from *John Constable's Correspondence*, vol II, published by the Record Society; 'Prayer Perfect' by Ervine Stenson and James Riley is reproduced with the kind permission of EMI Music Publishing.